KOREA

THE AIR WAR (2)

KOREA
THE AIR WAR (2)

Warren Thompson

OSPREY
AEROSPACE

Published in 1992 by
Osprey Publishing Limited
59 Grosvenor Street,
London W1X 9DA

ISBN 1 85532 234 X

Editor Dennis Baldry
Page design Colin Paine
Printed in Hong Kong

Front cover A flight of Checkertailed
North American F-86 Sabres from the
16th Fighter Interceptor Squadron
head back to Suwon Air Base (K-13)
after an uneventful patrol (as
indicated by the still-attached drop
tanks), over the extreme northern
edge of North Korea in early 1952.
Sabres of the 16th FIS were identified
by their blue tail trim (*Orland Jensen*)

Back cover Captain Jake Clements'
crew stand by *MOONSHINE*, their
Douglas B-26 Invader of the 8th
Bomb Squadron, at Kunsan AB (K-8).
The 8th BS was allocated yellow as
their colour code (*Jake Clements*)

Title page Tech Sgt George W
Glauser took this unusual shot of
Mount Fuji and his wingman flying
the photo version of the Grumman
Tigercat (F7F-3P) en route to a
mission over Korea in December
1950. This detachment of Marine
aircraft did the lion's share of photo
mapping the Inchon area for the
famous Inchon Landing. They were
assigned to operate under the control
of MAG-33 (*George Glauser*)

For a catalogue of all books published by Osprey Aerospace
please write to:

**The Marketing Department,
Octopus Illustrated Books, 1st Floor, Michelin House,
81 Fulham Road, London SW3 6RB**

Cat Girl, a 34th Bomb Squadron Douglas B-26 Invader, proves that low level attacks against the enemy can be hazardous. Note the battle damage to the plexiglas nose from ground fire. The 34th was assigned to the 17th Bomb Wing out of Pusan East (K-9) (*Dewey Albright*)

Introduction

For many years the American public's memory and awareness of the Korean War remained dormant. The Korean conflict broke out just too soon after World War 2, when everyone was starting to enjoy the good life.

For the United States Air Force, Marines and Navy, it was a test of putting a reduced regular force in with the Reserves and National Guard. Many were called up from civilian life after their skills as aviators had become somewhat rusty, but they brought themselves up to speed in a short period of time. Their efforts against the North Koreans and Chinese was nothing short of outstanding.

The US Air Force had just converted over to an all jet fighter force, which created tremendous problems during the early days of the war. The F-80s had to fly their missions from Japan as there were no air bases in South Korea suitable for jet operations. Their range allowed them only a few minutes over the target before they had to head back to base. To correct this problem, F-51 Mustangs were rushed from their Air National Guard units and brought to Japan. The Mustangs could loiter over any targets long enough to take them out and they could operate from crude runways. When large fuel tanks were fitted on the wing tips of the F-80s, they were also able to bring their heavy ordnance loads to bear on the enemy forces.

With the entry of the Soviet-built MiG-15 into the war, it was a good job the F-86 was available to counter the threat. The Sabre, as a gun platform, was second to none and many of the pilots were veterans from World War 2. As far as the Press was concerned, the public wanted to read about the dogfights and MiG kills. Meanwhile, the dirty war was being fought on the ground. The vast majority of UN aircraft were involved in either ground support or resupply. The air routes between Japan and South Korea must have seemed like the Los Angeles freeway.

The fighter bombers did an extraordinary job during the day. They hit the supply dumps, railroads and troop concentrations at a heavy loss to themselves. By mid-1951, the front lines had stabilized, somewhat, and then it became a cat and mouse game . . . played at night! The Chinese ran tens of thousands of trucks to the south in an effort to resupply and build up enough ammunition and food to support a major offensive. Most of these trucks never arrived at their destination. The B-26 crews and Marine F4U and F7F Night Fighters did an unbelievable job of destroying column after column of trucks in total darkness. Combining with this lethal group were the B-29s that flew the night missions far to the north, taking out major targets on the Yalu River. They sustained heavy losses from AAA and night flying MiGs. Their missions were long as they had to operate from bases at Yokota, Japan and Kadena, Okinawa.

Even though the Korean War was considered unpopular, it gave the United Nations credibility and it stopped the spread of communism into South Korea. It also made a statement on just how important airpower is if you have to go to war—a lesson demonstrated even more emphatically 40 years later in the Persian Gulf.

Hopefully, this Volume 2 will not be the final one as there are countless stories yet to be told on this war. If any reader has any material from Korea (1950–1953) please contact the author at 7201 Stamford Cove, Germantown, Tennessee 38138 USA.

Call Gal, a North American F-82G Twin Mustang assigned to the commanding officer of the 4th All Weather Squadron, Lt Col John Sharp, parked on the ramp at its home base of Naha AB, Okinawa. On 26 June 1950, this fighter was one of the first group of nine F-82s to be called into action by the 4th AWS. Two other squadrons from Okinawa would distinguish themselves during the early stages of the war; the 16th and 25th Fighter Squadrons (flying the F-80C) (*Cecil Marshall*)

Contents

F-51 Mustang

A North American F-51D Mustang of the 12th Fighter Bomber Squadron lifts off from its home base at Chinhae (K-10), probably en route to its forward operating location of Hoengsong (K-46). Most of the air cargo, petroleum products and ammunition flown into Korea arrived at Seoul City Airport (K-16), or Hoengsong, so the 18th Wing had to operate from an extremely crowded airfield. The big transports took a heavy toll on the runways, but the tractable Mustangs were able to carry on regardless (*James Harris*)

Captain Ernest F McDonald waits patiently in the cockpit of his F-51D while ground crews finish loading ordnance. This picture was taken at Seoul City Airport (K-16) in late 1950, when the front lines were deep into North Korea. Capt McDonald flew a total of 133 missions in Korea: 82 in the Mustang and the remaining 51 in the T-6 as a forward air controller. His fighter bears the name *Doris + 2*, for this wife and two children (*Ed Nebinger*)

Above Lt James Hambrick, a pilot with the 12th Fighter Bomber Squadron, poses by his F-51 at the unit's forward operating base (Hoengsong-K-46). At this period of the war (February 1952), the front lines were stabilized around the 38th parallel, so most of the missions flown by the 12th were against troop concentrations and ammunition dumps. The extreme cold did not slow down operations (*James Hambrick*)

Overleaf 'Blinker nose' Mustangs of the 39th Fighter Bomber Squadron parked on the flightline at Chinhae. Note the cargo carrier fitted to the wing pylon of aircraft '888. Fuselage stripes indicate that this is the squadron commander's personal mount. The 39th FBS converted to the F-86F Sabre jet fighter in June 1952 (*Glen Wold*)

Proud ground crew of F-51D *CLOSE SUPPORT* pose after preparing the fighter for another mission with a full ordnance load of 5 in rockets, 500 lb General-Purpose bombs and .50 cal machine gun rounds. This aircraft was assigned to the 39th Fighter Interceptor Squadron, 18th Fighter Bomber Wing. The base shown in this picture, Seoul, was only used temporarily as most of the 39th's missions were flown out of Chinhae (K-10) (*Robert Sandlin*)

Final preparations for a close support mission by a Mustang of the 67th Fighter Bomber Squadron. On this mission, no 500 lb GP bombs or rockets were to be used; the ground crew finish loading the napalm and .50 cal rounds while the pilot waits for the all-clear to start engines. The 67th FBS was controlled by the 18th Fighter Bomber Wing; this picture was taken at their main base at Chinhae (K-10) in the autumn of 1951 (*Max Tomich*)

Above Hurried maintenance on the 35th Fighter Bomber Squadron in September 1950, immediately after Kimpo airfield was captured during the UN counter-offensive in the wake of the 1st Marine Division's landing at Inchon. Operating bases changed on a weekly basis as the North Korean Army was pushed back under incessant air attack and artillery fire; ground crews worked around the clock to maintain high aircraft availability rates. Just a few weeks before the UN forces struck, the 35th FBS was still operating F-80 Shooting Stars from Itazuke AB, Japan (*Jim Tidwell*)

Below Lt Ed Haws returns from a mission over North Korea. Haws's unit, the 45th Tactical Reconnaissance Squadron, did most of the deep recon behind the front lines as the ground fire was so intense, the T-6 'Mosquito' was not allowed more than two miles behind the lines. At the beginning of the war most of the 45th's Mustangs were standard F-51D models, as the recce-dedicated RF-51s were in very limited supply (*Ed Haws*)

Below With the UN ground forces pushing the North Koreans almost back to the Yalu River, the Mustangs were delivering any type of ordnance they could get their hands on. This 35th Fighter-Bomber Squadron Mustang has obtained a couple of 'Tiny Tim' rockets from Marine stocks and is prepared for a mission to the north from Kimpo Air Base in early November 1950 (*Frank Clark*)

Above A flight of four 67th Fighter Bomber Squadron F-51s prepare to launch on a close support mission out of Chinhae sometime in 1952. Major Louis J Sebille, a commander of the 67th early on in the war, received the Medal of Honor when he deliberately crashed his Mustang into a concentration of enemy trucks and troops after taking several hits from ground fire. One of his 500 lb bombs hung up in the attack and he tried to make one more pass to shake it free; he died instantly in the explosion (*John Justus*)

The 18th Fighter Bomber Wing were second to none in the ground attack role. The Commander of the 5th Air Force, General Partridge, called the 18th FBW 'the ace truck-busters of the 5th AF'. Operating from Chinhae, each individual unit in the Wing designed and made its own patches, the chosen theme being *Dogpatch/Lil' Abner* cartoon characters (*Steve Lavandoski*)

Major maintenance is performed on a 45th Tactical Recon Squadron Mustang under the crudest of conditions as a group of retired South Korean farmers go about their business near the village of Chungu. In the early weeks of 1951, the 45th TRS took tremendous punishment from Chinese ground fire because of the need to fly at extremely low altitude. This picture was taken in April 1951 (*Bill Disbrow*)

F-80 Shooting Star

Flight of Lockheed F-80 Shooting Stars from the 8th Fighter Bomber Squadron return from a mission over North Korea in May 1951. Based at Taegu AB (K-2) and controlled by the 49th Fighter Bomber Wing, the 8th FBS flew their F-80s very hard, but the ground crews still managed to maintain an overall aircraft in-commission rate approaching 85 per cent (*Budd Butcher*)

Right Lt Budd Butcher poses beside his F-80 of the 8th FBS after a long mission up north. The conditions at Taegu were crude at best; the runways had been expanded over former rice paddies with pierced steel planks (PSP), producing an irregular surface which required constant maintenance and upgrading (*Budd Butcher*)

Below F-80 *Kansas Tornado*, assigned to the 16th Fighter Bomber Squadron, being serviced by its ground crew in preparation for another mission. Lt Colonel Ben Warren, the squadron commander, poses beside one of his fighters in South Korea. The 16th and 25th Squadrons deployed to Itazuke AB from their base at Naha AB, Okinawa on 22 September 1950 and flew in combat the same day (*Bill Williams*)

Tight quarters and a dangerous place to work! 7th Fighter Bomber Squadron F-80 crews work among 500 lb and 1000 lb bombs along with an assortment of napalm tanks as they ready their aircraft for rapid turnaround. This shot was taken at Taegu in late-spring 1951, when the Chinese were still using 'human wave' tactics—though the front lines were becoming stable (*Budd Butcher*)

Pilots of the 80th Fighter Bomber Squadron strapping in for a mission to the north. The ground crews are still working on the aircraft as they prepare to taxi at Suwon AB. This picture was taken in 1951 before the sandbag revetments were built. From this period on, the F-86 equipped 51st Fighter Wing and the F-80 equipped 8th Fighter Bomber Wing would use Suwon (K-13) as their main operating base (*W G Sieber*)

Below An 8th Fighter Bomber Squadron F-80, loaded and ready to go, just a few days after the squadron moved its operations from Itazuke AB to Taegu (K-2). All three squadrons of the 49th Fighter Bomber Group moved into South Korea on the 28, 29 and 30 September 1950—the first jet-equipped TFG to operate from South Korean soil. The squadron's black sheep emblem is visible on the nose of the fighter (*Allen Nelson*)

Above A 15th Tactical Reconnaissance Squadron RF-80A eases out of its revetment at Kimpo for another photo mission deep into North Korea. The RF-80A was too slow to fly the mission unescorted as the MiG-15 could catch it easily. They were usually escorted by 4th Fighter Wing F-86 Sabres, conveniently based at the same airfield. Numerous sorties were flown each day to determine the selection of targets for the fighter-bombers on the following day (*Gene Newnam*)

Above Lt Col Levi R Chase, commander of the 8th Fighter Bomber Group, talks with his crew chief before strapping into the cockpit for a rail-cutting mission. On 11 March, the 8th Group flew 254 sorties with 51 Shooting Stars against ammunition dumps in the Mulgae-ri area (*Richard Durkee*)

Right Lt Col Clure Smith, commanding officer of the 25th Fighter Squadron, returning from a mission over the north in late October 1950. The 51st Fighter Wing sent two of its squadrons to fight in Korea (16th and 25th). They arrived at Itazuke on 22 September and flew in combat the same day. The markings on this F-80 indicate that it was flown by the Wing Commander from Naha AB, Okinawa (*Boyd Gibson*)

Right 2nd Lt Clarence H Hoggard taxies out from the 36th Squadron flightline with a full load of ordnance. This was to be Hoggard's 100th mission in Korea (3 January 1952). The squadron still had over a year to go before they would trade in their F-80s for new F-86F Sabres (*Clarence H Hoggard*)

Left Early stages of another harsh Korean winter—light snow on the flightline at Suwon (K-13) in late 1952. The red sunburst on the tails of these F-80C's indicate assignment to the 36th Fighter Bomber Squadron. Note the distant fighter with the blue trim from the 35th Fighter Bomber Squadron, a sister unit of the 36th's and 80th's. Both the 35th and 36th squadrons operated the F-51D, F-80C and F-86F during the war (*Tom Owen*)

"NEW HEAD" "50 MISSIONS" "90 MISSIONS!"

Left Every Operations Room, Mess Hall, etc, was never lacking for cartoons and murals depicting life in each squadron; the 8th Fighter Bomber Group was no exception. This colourful sketch of a typical fighter pilot was displayed in the 80th Fighter Bomber Squadron's Ops building at Suwon, South Korea (*Frank Ray*)

Top right Frank Ray stands by his F-80, *6 GUNS FOR HIRE*, at Suwon. The 'Headhunters' of the 80th FBS always carried yellow trim on their fighters. The unit operated the F-80 during the early days of the war while its two sister squadrons (35th and 36th) switched over to the F-51D for a short period. The 80th FBS logged more F-80 time than any other squadron in the Korean War (*Frank Ray*)

Right 8th Fighter Bomber Wing commanding officer's personal mount; despite the primitive conditions, the ground crews maintained the aircraft in immaculate order. The colourful paint scheme represents all three of the Wing's squadrons. This aircraft was flown by various pilots from the other units and received no special treatment (*Frank Ray*)

F-84
Thunderjet

Two Republic F-84 Thunderjets from the 7th Fighter Bomber Squadron fly close formation while returning from a mission into North Korea, sometime in 1952. The 7th, one of three squadrons in the 49th Fighter Bomber Wing, flew F-80s early in the war (*Bill Boland*)

Below Russ Knoebel, a pilot in the 311th Fighter Bomber Squadron, took this fine study of an F-84 Thunderjet as it returned from bombing and strafing supply lines up north. Domination of the air by the UN forces made it extremely hazardous for the enemy to transport fuel, ammunition and rations in daylight—very little got through to the front line troops except at night (*Russ Knoebel*)

Above F-84 of the 524th Fighter Bomber Squadron begins its take-off roll at Taegu. Note the F-80s of the 49th Fighter-Bomber Group across the field. The condition of the runway had deteriorated since the summer months due to extremely high utilization (*Allen Nelson*)

Overleaf An F-84 from the 8th Fighter Bomber Squadron hauls its bombs up north sometime in 1952, probably on a rail cutting mission. On several occasions, larger numbers of Thunderjets provided flak suppression for B-29 Superfortresses when they bombed the big Pyongyang Downtown Airfield (*Don James*)

A 'boss bird' F-84 Thunderjet of the 474th Fighter Bomber Wing fully-armed and ready for action on the ramp at Taegu shortly before the war ended. The CO of the 474th FBW was Colonel John Loisel, one of the leading P-38 Lightning pilots in World War 2, who flew with the famous 475th Fighter Group, 'Satan's Angels' (*I J Pierce*)

F-84 Thunderjets lined up at Taegu in June 1952. The yellow trim indicates their assignment to the 154th Fighter Bomber Squadron, 136th Fighter Bomber Wing. The 136th FBW started replacing the 27th Fighter Escort Wing, squadron by squadron, from early June 1951, and the transition was completed by 1 August 1951. The three squadrons in the Wing were made up of two Texas Air National Guard units and the 154th FBS from Little Rock, Arkansas (*Cale Herry*)

Below Lt Leland Speakes, a pilot in the 430th Fighter Bomber Squadron, prepares to start the turbojet of his F-84 for an interdiction mission against Chinese supply lines. This picture was taken at Kunsan AB in January 1953, right in the middle of the bitterly cold Korean winter (*Leland Speakes*)

Above An F-84 undergoing routine maintenance after a mission. This aircraft was assigned to the 474th Fighter Bomber Wing operating out of Kunsan. The Wing participated in strikes against the 'Kumgang Political School' at Odong-ni on 25 October 1952. The school was instructing 1000 students for subversive activities in South Korea. The raid was massive, using 84 aircraft from the 49th, 58th and 474th Fighter Bomber Wings (*Bob Gilliland*)

Below *DELECTIBLE DEE*, an F-84 flown by Lt Randy Presley, parked on the 428th Fighter Bomber Squadron flightline at Taegu (K-2) in June 1953. With only one month to go before the end of the war, the F-84's were constantly in the air, pounding North Korean airfields. With the truce near, it was necessary to prevent the enemy from bringing in their aircraft from China, thus the heavy emphasis on these targets (*Randy Presley*)

Above The Korean winters are some of the coldest in the world. Here ground crews brave the elements to load 500 lb bombs after a heavy snow fall at Taegu. These F-84s were assigned to the 69th Fighter Bomber Squadron of the 58th Fighter Bomber Wing. When the 136th Fighter Group was moved out of Korea, the 58th FBW took over their aircraft. The blue-tailed F-84s of the 69th FBS had previously been operated by the 111th FBS (*Al Schneider*)

Above *RICE PADDY RANGER*, an F-84 assigned to 2nd Lt Quinn Fuller of the
8th Fighter Bomber Squadron at Taegu, waits for the ordnance crews who will
prepare it for tomorrow's mission. In December 1952, the 8th's sister squadron,
the 9th FBS, was withdrawn from Korea and sent to Japan for training in the
delivery of tactical nuclear weapons, and would not return to combat
(*Quinn Fuller*)

Below A new F-84G assigned to the 8th Fighter Bomber Squadron ready for a mission up north. This Thunderjet was flown by Lt Charles Scofield. The 8th's parent unit, the 49th FBW, was the first to receive its full complement of 'G' models; conversion began in August 1952 and was completed in October that same year (*Charles Scofield*)

Right Colonel Joe Davis's Thunderjet being refuelled for another trip up north. The colourful paint scheme represented all the colours of the three squadrons in the wing. The emblem painted on the right side below the canopy is that of the 430th Fighter Bomber Squadron (*Chester Lamb*)

Left Early morning at Kunsan and ground crews of the 474th Fighter Bomber Group prepare their F-84s for the upcoming mission. Most of the maintenance and ordnance loading was done out in the open, exposed to the elements. Kunsan was right on the ocean and experienced extremely harsh winters. This big base was home for the 474th FBS, a B-26 Wing (3rd) and the Marine Night Fighter Squadron (*H A Gamblin*)

F-86 Sabre

North American F-86 Sabres of the 16th Fighter Interceptor Squadron on the prowl over North Korea at the beginning of 1952, a few months before the controlling 51st Wing added checkertails to their aircraft (see front cover). Colonel Francis S Gabreski, the renowned P-47 Thunderbolt ace from World War 2, took command of the 51st Wing in early November 1951 as it transitioned from the Lockheed F-80C Shooting Star to the F-86 (*Richard Schoeneman*)

Above Cartoon characters painted on the Sabres were plentiful near the end of the war. Here, pilot Lt Dick Weghorn, of the 16th Fighter Interceptor Squadron stands beside his *Pluto* chasing a MiG-15. This aircraft has the checkertail of the 51st Fighter Wing (*Dick Weghorn*)

Below A/2C Earl Shutt rests on the wing of his Sabre, *MIGHTY MOUSE* after preparing it for the next mission. His job as crew chief meant long hours on the flight line. The name on the port side of this famous F-86 was *MIG MASTER*. This aircraft was assigned to the 39th Fighter Interceptor Squadron at K-13 *(Earl Shutt)*

Captain Cliff Jolley talks with his crew chief, Sgt Ernie Balasz, about the performance of his *JOLLEY ROGER*. Capt Jolley became the 18th jet ace in the Korean War and finished his combat tour with seven confirmed MiG kills, all of which were made while he was assigned to the 335th Fighter Interceptor Squadron (*Cliff Jolley*)

A crowd at Kimpo gathers around Capt Cliff Jolley as he pulls into his parking slot after another intense air combat mission against the MiG-15s. Note the damage on the left wing—the second time Jolley had taken hits from enemy fighters (*Karl Dittmer*)

A group of 25th Fighter Interceptor Squadron pilots and flight surgeon pose while relaxing in between missions. On the far left is Lt Harry Shumate, second from left is the Group's Flight Surgeon Major Bernard Brungardt. Second from the right is pilot Lt Joe Cannon and on the far right is the 10th jet ace of the war, Captain Ivan Kincheloe. One of Kincheloe's MiG kills was made while protecting Joe Cannon, who had been shot down (*Doc San Brungardt*)

A 25th Fighter Interceptor Squadron F-86 receives detailed attention from the maintenance crews in an effort to keep all of the aircraft mission ready. By 1952 MiGs were extremely active and dogfights were numerous over the Yalu. The 'E' models given to the 51st Fighter Interceptor Wing fared very well against its speedy adversary (*Joe Cannon*)

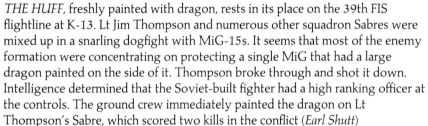

THE HUFF, freshly painted with dragon, rests in its place on the 39th FIS flightline at K-13. Lt Jim Thompson and numerous other squadron Sabres were mixed up in a snarling dogfight with MiG-15s. It seems that most of the enemy formation were concentrating on protecting a single MiG that had a large dragon painted on the side of it. Thompson broke through and shot it down. Intelligence determined that the Soviet-built fighter had a high ranking officer at the controls. The ground crew immediately painted the dragon on Lt Thompson's Sabre, which scored two kills in the conflict (*Earl Shutt*)

An impressive line up of 25th FIS F-86E models at their base at K-13. This shot
was taken just a few weeks before the end of the war. The 25th FIS would go
on to distinguish itself in the Vietnam war flying F-4 Phantom IIs
(*Hank Buttelmann*)

A perfect row of F-86Fs of the 36th Fighter Bomber Squadron at their base at K-13, spring 1953. The 36th FBS was the first of the 8th's squadrons to convert from the F-80C to the F-86F, beginning the process on 22 February 1953; it went very smoothly as all of the pilots had jet experience and remained at K-13 for some time (*Dick Seger*)

Lt Joe Lynch's F-86F, *Miss Whiteville*, sits on the end of the 35th Fighter Bomber Squadron ramp at K-13 in summer of 1953. Note the 8th Fighter Bomber Wing's hack C-47 in the distance with tail colours of all three squadrons displayed. The blue colour code was assigned to the 35th Squadron. Very few of the Wing's aircraft were able to get into the MiGs as they were heavily committed to close air support behind the front line positions (*Joe Lynch*)

Lt Bob McDermott confers with this crew chief prior to flying a mission. The yellow trim on the tail shows that this Sabre was assigned to the 80th Fighter Bomber Squadron. The 80th FBS did not stand down for the conversion from the F-80C until 1 May 1953, so they were the last squadron to receive the F-86F before the war ended (*Robert McDermott*)

It must have been a day when there were no MiGs in the air. The entire roster of officers assigned to the 25th Fighter Interceptor Squadron pose for a squadron picture at K-13. Capt Ivan Kincheloe is on the back row fourth from the left (*Joe Cannon*)

Above A 335th Fighter Interceptor Squadron F-86 waits on the alert pad for a possible scramble; Lt Richard Keener is the pilot. Note the colourful 335th FIS emblem painted on the side of the aircraft. All of the 4th Fighter Interceptor Wing Sabres had their respective squadron emblems painted on them (*Dick Keener*)

Below Lt Bruno Giordano of the 334th Fighter Interceptor Squadron poses in his Sabre at K-14. Note the massive effort to protect the aircraft from an air attack. The revetments at K-14 were much higher than the aircraft with only the tips of the tails showing. The threat of large-scale attacks on K-13 and K-14 never materialized, but 'Bed Check Charlies' pulled off several nuisance raids (*Bruno Giordano*)

Below Parked in revetments at Suwon, Sabres of the 25th Fighter Interceptor Squadron wait for their turn to hunt the MiGs. *AUNT MYRNA* was assigned to Walt Copeland, who took this superb photo.

Above *GOPHER LOAFER*, an F-86F assigned to the 67th Fighter Bomber
Squadron, is prepared for another sortie over the front lines from its superbase
at Osan (K-55) in the summer of 1953. The squadron operated the F-51
Mustang for most of the war, converting to the F-86 in early 1953 (*Vic Collier*)

B-29 Superfortress

Nose art on the Boeing B-29 Superfortress was much more pronounced than on any other type of aircraft in Korea. The *LEMON DROP KID* was named in honour of American comedian Bob Hope. Hope's contributions to the morale of the American military in World War 2 and Korea were considerable. Based at Kadena AFB, Japan, this B-29 of the 19th Bomb Group made its presence known over enemy targets in North Korea (*John Johnson*)

One of the many B-29s of the 19th Group displays its nine missions under the cockpit. The red fins on the bomb symbols indicate missions in which the bomber took flak hits. On 30 June 1950, B-29s of the 19th Bomb Group hit the massive troop formations along the north bank of the Han River with 260 lb fragmentation bombs. It was the first decisive strike flown by the Superforts in the war. Shown on the right is Sgt Jim Stark, one of the crew chiefs in the Group (*Jim Stark*)

The B-29s were called into action as early as 28 June 1950 when Twentieth Air Force was ordered to move its bombers from Guam to Kadena Air Base. They would immediately dispatch them against targets of opportunity. *My Assam Dragon III* typifies the quality of the Air Force's amateur artistry (*John Johnson*)

Right *SOUTH SEA SINNER*, one of the 19th Bomb Group's B-29s, rests at its base on Okinawa between missions over North Korea. In mid-July 1950, fifty B-29s of the 19th, 92nd and 22nd Bomb Groups hit Wonsan Oil Refinery, dock areas and marshalling yards with over 500 tons of high explosive bombs. Aerial photos taken after the strike showed massive damage to the targets (*Jim Stark*)

Left A recently arrived B-29 gets its underside prepared for the black camouflage paint job before flying in combat at night over North Korea. This picture was taken on Kadena by 19th BG pilot Lt Louis Branch

Right This 30th Bomb Squadron B-29 was equipped to carry the 12,000 lb 'Tarzon' bomb which was guided to its target by radio signals sent out by the aircraft's bombardier. It proved to be a fairly accurate weapon with tremendous destructive power. On 13 January 1951 a single B-29 dropped a Tarzon bomb from 15,000 ft, scoring a direct hit on a railway bridge at Kanggye, dropping it into the water (*George Amthor*)

Below The bombers had to contend with heavy AAA over the target and night flying MiG-15s, which would stalk them into the target and wait for them to head home after the bomb drop. This B-29 had both left engines shot up by MiGs, forcing the aircraft to make an emergency landing at Kimpo AB, South Korea. Note that both of the props are still feathered. Curious Air Force personnel are gathered around the aircraft. B-29s were not often seen on the ground in Korea as they operated from bases on Okinawa and mainland Japan (*William J O'Donnell*)

Above A B-29 assigned to the 98th Bomb Group lands at Itazuke, Japan sometime in 1952. Both the 307th and 98th Bomb Groups received orders to move into the war on 1 August 1950. The former launched its first combat strike from Kadena on 8 August, exactly one week after it had left its home base in Florida (*Lynn Balow*)

Below *CAPTAIN SAM & TEN SCENTS* was, most probably, the most elaborately painted B-29 operating out of Kadena with the 19th Bomb Group. The first four B-29s to fly over Korea after the war started were told to fly over certain highways north of Seoul and randomly bomb any targets that were available. Two of the bombers covered the road and railroad between Seoul and Kapyong and the other two covered the same between Seoul and Uijongbu (*John Johnson*)

Right Maintenance on the big World War 2 bombers was never ending. Ground crews of the 93rd Bomb Squadron service their B-29 on Kadena in 1952. On 28 March 1952, the B-29s dropped their 100,000th ton of bombs in the war. The mission that accomplished this feat was against the big rail bridge at Chongju (*Chuck Baisden*)

Left *"MARGIE'S MADGREEK!"* III, a B-29 assigned to the 19th Bomb Group, parked at Kadena AB. During the early days of the war when the UN forces were backed up in the Pusan Perimeter, a few B-29s were assigned to drop M-26 parachute flares that would ignite at 6000 ft. The B-26s would be in a position to work the roads under the flares, destroying several trains and trucks (*Griff Jones*)

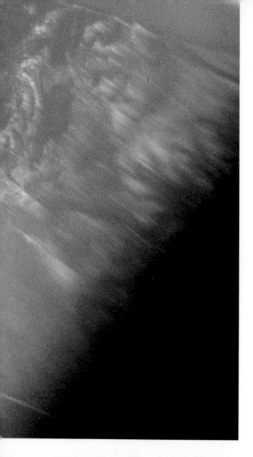

One of the most dramatic pictures taken from a B-29 shows the bombs hitting Taechon Air Field (North Korea) on 22 October 1951. This was a major base for the communists as indicated by the number of revetments. The bombs have been well placed along the main runway (*Chuck Baisden*)

Many of the B-29s were shot up so badly over the targets that they could not make it back to their bases. Taegu (K-2) and Kimpo (K-14) air bases were used frequently by the damaged 'forts. This 98th Bomb Group aircraft had to crash land at Taegu as a result of severe battle damage. To their credit B-29 gunners achieved numerous 'kills'—on 27 October 1951 they destroyed six MiG-15s. However, heavy enemy fighter activity forced Bomber Command to switch to night operations exclusively on 29 October 1951 (*Allen Miller*)

Overleaf Formation of B-29s en route from their base at Kadena to bomb the Taechon, North Korea area 1951. The bomber shown in the picture was assigned to the 93rd Bomb Squadron. October 1951 was hazardous for the B-29s as enemy fighter efforts tripled against them. As many as 200 MiGs came up against the formations in a single battle. On 24 October, three B-29s were lost to these fighters while bombing Namsi (*Chuck Baisden*)

B-26 Invader

Left Lt LeRoy Bain, a pilot in the 13th Bomb Squadron, poses in the cockpit of his Douglas B-26 Invader. During the first few days of the war, B-26s from the 3rd Bomb Group made the initial bomb strikes against the North Koreans. The roads were glutted with enemy tanks, trucks etc. The '26s inflicted heavy damage, but their numbers were not great enough to slow the advancing North Koreans (*LeRoy Bain*)

Below *BROWN NOSE*, a B-26 assigned to the 730th Bomb Squadron, displays its .50 cal firepower—bad news for enemy truck columns at night. Once the bombers had dropped their bombs and started numerous fires along the roads, they would come back with all eight .50's blazing, causing heavy casualties among convoy personnel and triggering huge secondary explosions . . . (*Robert Stoner*)

Two 90th Bomb Squadron B-26s make a daylight formation bomb drop over North Korea during the summer of 1952. The photo was snapped by Sgt Gary Long. The 90th BS was identified by the white trim painted on the aircraft. On 25 June 1951, the 731st Bomb Squadron was inactivated and the 90th Bomb Squadron (Light) was activated and assigned to the 3rd Bomb Wing (*Gary Long*)

Below Gary Long works on his .50 calibre Browning machine guns in the dorsal turret as the B-26 is prepared for a night interdiction mission over North Korea. Long's machine carries the white trim of the 90th Bomb Squadron, while the Invader in the background is marked with the red trim of the 13th Bomb Squadron; both units were assigned to the 3rd Bomb Wing at Kunsan AB (K-8) (*Gary Long*)

Right Living proof of just how tough it could be! A 452nd Bomb Group B-26 limps home on 3 May 1951 with its nose shattered and the right engine feathered after taking intense ground fire on low level mission (*Robert Stoner*)

Bottom right 13th Bomb Squadron B-26 *Louise* sits on the ramp at Kunsan in the spring of 1953. This aircraft was assigned to Captain Allan Scholz. In August 1952, most of the B-26 squadrons were redirected to concentrate on communications centres. However, the 13th Squadron was chosen to continue night-intruder missions. They would be limited to a 4000 ft minimum altitude when bombing targets (*Allan Scholz*)

Below An enviable record is displayed by ol' No 940. Unfortunately, this veteran warhorse came to a tragic end later in the war. On a ferry flight to Japan in bad weather it struck the side of a hill on landing approach, killing the pilot and mechanic on board (*Clarence Klenk*)

Above Radar maintenance shack at Kunsan (K-8). Without a good sense of humour all would have been lost in such an unpopular war. The mascot for the 13th Bomb Squadron was 'Oscar', a skeletal caricature. When the war started the squadron was on duty in Japan—within three days they were flying in combat over South Korea (*LeRoy Bain*)

Top left A rare daytime picture of a 12th Tactical Recon Squadron RB-26 in flight as they were strictly nocturnal. This shot was taken in August 1951 close to Suwon. The home base for the 12th was Kimpo (K-14) as they were part of the 67th Tactical Recon Wing. It was very difficult to locate and photograph targets at night. The RB-26s were able to use Shoran to get an accurate fix, but when operating over the north with its mountainous terrain they had to fly at higher altitudes to receive the Shoran and would be too high over the target to get good pictures (*Al Wilkerson*)

Left Flightline at Kimpo (K-14) on the 67th TRW ramp. These RB-26s were assigned to the 12th Tactical Recon Squadron. The 12th operated the RB-26 for the length of the war while its two sister squadrons, the 45th and 15th TRS, flew the RF-51/RF-80 and RF-80/RF-86 respectively. These three squadrons did the lion's share of recon work in Korea. The Marines also contributed significantly with their Banshee recce birds. Note the old Kimpo Air Terminal in the background (*George Ballweg*)

Above 1st Lt Clarence Klenk of the 90th Bomb Squadron has his picture taken with another veteran of the Korean conflict, ol' 940. This Invader flew the 3rd Bomb Wing's 10,000th sortie on 19 June 1951 and went to to rack up the 20,000th on 21 June 1952 (*Clarence Klenk*)

Above right Sgt H Allen Gamblin, a B-26 flight engineer with the 90th Bomb Squadron, poses in front of his beloved *Delores* at Kunsan AB (*H Allen Gamblin*)

Right One of the more colourful B-26s (*AHAULIN ASS*) is shown parked on the ramp at its base at K-9 in 1952. On 20 July 1952, the 3rd and 17th Bomb Wings started hitting communist communication centres with M-20 incendiary clusters and M-76 fire bombs. These raids produced excellent results (*St Clair Thompson*)

Navy/Marine Airpower

On February 1951, two Marine night fighter squadrons were consolidated into one. VMF(N)-513 would prove to be one of the largest fighter squadrons in recent history with fifteen Vought F4U-5N Corsairs and fifteen Grumman F7F-3N Tigercats. Their night interdiction missions became legendary. This picture of VMF(N)-513 pilots was taken in April 1951 along with their respective fighter aircraft. VMF(N)-542 would be moved back to the states to convert over to the new Douglas F3D Skynight (*Ray Stewart*)

An unusual sight . . . a Marine F7F-3N Tigercat and F4U-5N Corsair from VMF(N)-513, and a 68th All Weather Squadron F-82 share night alert duties at Suwon in the autumn of 1951. Although the F-82 was replaced by the F-94, the two Marine aircraft flew night interdiction for a considerable period and proved to be extremely effective (*Charles Toler*)

Left VMF(N)-542 flightline at Kimpo AB in October 1950. The squadron had become operational in the war on 23 September. The F7F Tigercat could carry two 500 lb bombs, eight 5 in rockets and a 300 US gal fuel tank slung under its belly. With full load of ordnance the aircraft had an endurance of four hours, making it ideal for close support or long interdiction missions. With UN ground forces pushing north, the F7F could easily reach the Yalu River on its missions. (*Al Wimer*)

Below Night fighter Corsairs lined up on the flight line at K-1 (Pusan) in April 1951. These VMF(N)-513 aircraft were very effective at working with the flare ships over North Korea at night. The loss of equipment and supplies by the Chinese to the F4Us, F7Fs and B-26s was astronomical. Due to the number of UN aircraft in the air during the day, the communists had to move their supplies by night, making the night fighter's role even more important (*Ray Stewart*)

Right Radar Operator, Captain E J Lloyd, took this picture of VMF(N)-513 F3D Skynights lined up at Kunsan AB in late 1952. These state of the art night fighters flew with the B-29s on their missions during the hours of darkness and stopped the MiG-15s from inflicting any damage on the bombers. The Skynights scored several MiG 'kills' before the war ended (*E J Lloyd*)

Left A plane captain for VMF-214 in the process of preparing his Corsair for the next mission. In August 1950, '214 and '323 were one of the first Marine squadrons to be sent into the war. Both units, were initially responsible for supporting the 1st Provisional Marine Brigade. Note the famous 'black sheep' emblem painted on the nose of the Corsair (*Clarence Chick*)

Corsairs of VMF-312 loading up with ordnance aboard the USS *Bairoko* somewhere off the coast of North Korea in 1952. On 20 September 1950, the 'Checkerboards' flew their first combat mission from Kimpo AB; they would be in the thick of combat until replaced by VMF-332 in June 1953. On 1 December 1950, the squadron moved far to the north and flew out of Yonpo Air Base at Hamhung until the Chinese entered the war and forced all of the UN aircraft south of the 38th parallel (*Stu Nelson*)

Lt Colonel Russ Janson takes time out to pose by his Goodyear-built AU-1 Corsair under adverse weather conditions. This aircraft was noted for its high performance and was respected by its pilots. VMF-212 had the privilege of flying these fighters during the Korean War. Janson's AU-1 has already been armed and will fly regardless of the cold or snow (*Russ Janson*)

A little R&R never hurt anyone! VMA-332 crews and personnel enjoy the entertainment provided while docked at a base in Japan during the summer of 1953. Note that the aircraft were in the process of changing from the checkerboard cowling to the polka dots (*Jim Hallet*)

The WS tail codes indicate that these are VMF-323 'Death Rattler' Corsairs. Early on, the squadron had the Rattler painted on the cowling, but as time went on this practice was dropped. This picture was taken about the USS *Sicily* in 1951 (*Conrad Buschman*)

Corsairs from the 'Polka Dots' ... VMA-332 line up at Kunsan during the
summer of 1953. VMA-332 replaced the 'Checkerboard' squadron (VMA-312)
about six weeks before the war ended. They flew their combat missions from
the USS *Bairoko*. Colonel Jack Berteling, CO of VMA-332, notes from his
logbook that the first operational flight from the carrier was on 18 June 1953.
VMA-332 was the sixth Marine F4U squadron to see combat in Korea
(*H A Gamblin*)

A very rare picture of VMF-212 Corsairs over North Korea with full load of bombs. Note the austere, cold appearance of the mountains below. This dramatic shot was taken by squadron pilot, E H 'Ace' Yeager, flying off the right wing of the formation (E H Yeager)

Above On 30 November 1950, VMF-311 unloaded its Grumman F9F Panthers from the USS *Bairoko* at Kizarazu, Japan. One week later, the first VMF-311 aircraft departed Japan for Yonpo Airfield (K-27) deep into North Korea. At 1640 hours on 10 December, the squadron flew its first combat strike—the debut of Marine jet aircraft in combat (*Fred Krause*)

Below When the USS *Boxer* brought the initial load of F-51 Mustangs to the region shortly after the Korean War began, the carrier also deployed a lethal load of Navy aircraft. A Navy Grumman F9F Panther is shown on the deck with one of the Mustangs. It was on 18 November 1950 that the Navy F9Fs first tangled with the MiG-15s over Sinuiju (*Ray Carnahan*)

In the spring of 1953, this US Navy Panther was parked at K-14 for a brief visit. Both the Navy's AD and the F9F were workhorses for the Navy during the Korean War. On 24/25 June 1952, 35 F9F's from the USS *Boxer, Princeton* and *Philippine Sea* attacked the big generating plant at Sui-ho. This raid included scores of other UN aircraft types and was rated as a tremendous success (*Harry Jones*)

VMF-115 Panthers carrying a heavy load of bombs wait for their pilots while operating out of K-13. They were the equivalent of the Air Force's F-80. The unidentified pilot standing by the Panther is an F-80 pilot from the 8th Group (*Charles Rowan*)

A classic example of the support that the Douglas AD-1 Skyraider could provide for ground troops. This big fighter-bomber from VMA-121 is parked at its base at Pyongtaek (K-6) in September 1952. Marine Air Group 12 (MAG-12) operated out of this base with its AD's and Corsairs. It was located about thirty miles southeast of Inchon (*Harry Pierkowski*)

A Marine AD Skyraider assigned to VMA-121 parked at the big Marine base at K-6. Not only could this fighter-bomber carry a heavy bomb load, but it had excellent loiter time over the target area—a boon to Forward Air Controllers (*Al Fulford*)

They Also Served

A North American RB-45 Tornado photographed on the ramp at Osan AB (K-55) in the early spring of 1953. On 31 January 1951, Reconnaissance Detachment A of the 84th Bombardment Squadron deployed a pair of RB-45s for tests in the Korean Theatre. Subsequently attached to the 91st Strategic Recon Squadron, the Tornados were often jumped by MiGs, who would apparently continue to blaze away at them until their ammo was expended. Only poor marksmanship on the part of the MiG pilots saved the Tornado crews (*Charles Gelveles*)

Below Usually the 319th FIS operated out of K-13, but this F-94B was parked at Kunsan (K-8) in early 1953. The C-119 in the background was one of the many aircraft that were constantly in the air between Korea and Japan. The F-94s of the 319th FIS replaced the F-94s and F-82s of the 68th All-Weather Squadron to provide air defence for the Air Force in Korea during the hours of darkness (*Al Gamblin*)

Above Before the 319th FIS was deployed from the states to assume the all weather responsibility, the 68th All Weather Squadron out of Itazuke pulled alert at Suwon (K-13). These two Lockheed F-94B Starfires are shown on the alert pad (*Al Farnsworth*)

Right Lt Les Bjorklund, a 'Mosquito' pilot in the 6147th Tactical Control Group, poses by his North American T-6G Texan at the Chunchon base. T-6G pilots marked most of the targets for fighter bomber aircraft in Korea, working with just about every F/B type during the conflict. When hard pressed ground troops saw the 'Mosquito' arrive on the scene, they knew that help was just ' minutes away (*Les Bjorklund*)

Below Forward Air Control on the ground was dangerous to say the least, but it had to be done. Fighter pilots were required to spend a certain amount of time close to the front. They would talk to their fellow pilots, giving them vital information as to where the targets were located, etc. This FAC is a fighter pilot from the 8th Fighter Bomber Group during the early days in 1950 when they were flying the Mustang over South Korea (*William O'Donnell*)

Above On 27 September 1951, a single Douglas C-124 Globemaster was sent to Japan for service tests. It made 26 flights between Japan and Korea carrying an average load of 34,400 lb. This was about twice the load hauled by the C-54s. Not surprisingly, the timetable for the conversion of the 374th Troop Carrier Wing from the C-54 to the C-124 was moved up. This Globemaster is unloading its cargo and refuelling for the flight back to Japan ... Seoul City Airport (K-16) in spring of 1953 (*Lloyd Irish*)

Below Supplies were essential to the UN effort in Korea, and it all had to be brought in by air or water. These C-119's were kept in the air as much as their maintenance would allow. Due to the engine shortages and other problems, the C-119s were able to achieve a utilization rate of 100 hours per month. These aircraft worked closely with the 187th Airborne Regimental Combat Team on several paradrops in Korea (*George J Busher*)

Right After the Inchon Landing and the North Korean army was collapsing, the push north to the Yalu River was in full swing. Most of the airpower was operating from bases north of the 38th parallel. The ground troops however, were meeting tough pockets of resistance and taking casualties. This Douglas C-54 Skymaster is taking on wounded at a captured base near the North Korean capital of Pyongyang. They are being flown back to Japan for medical attention (*William O'Donnell*)

Bottom left The Australians were quick to join the United Nations efforts with the commitment of 26 F-51 Mustangs on 29 June 1950. No 77 Sqn would remain in the war for the duration. In July 1951, the squadron received Gloster Meteor F.8 jets and would use them until the war's end, while attached to the 4th Fighter Wing at Kimpo (K-14). This rare picture shows both aircraft types flown by the Aussies parked at Pusan (*George J Busher*)

Below RAAF Meteor F.8 assigned to No 77 Sqn is shown parked in the snow at Suwon in early 1953. The straight wing Meteor was never an even match for the swept wing MiG-15 and when the 8th and 18th Fighter Bomber Wings traded their F-51s for the new F-86F Sabres, the Meteors were able to concentrate more on the fighter-bomber role. The 'F' model Sabre had the same job, but were capable of giving the MiGs more than they bargained for (*Gerald McIlmoyle*)

An H-19 rescue helicopter goes over some evasion and survival practice with fighter pilots of the 18th Fighter Bomber Wing at K-46. This knowledge allowed numerous pilots to escape from behind enemy lines (*Richard Keener*)

Above Royal Navy Supermarine Seafire FR.47 and a Fairey Firefly FR.5 rest on the ramp at Itazuke Air Base, Japan during the summer of 1950. These aircraft types along with the Hawker Sea Fury did yeoman service in the ground attack role flying from British carriers off the coast of North Korea. Itazuke was the home base of the 8th Fighter Bomber Wing before the war started (*Fletcher Meadows*)

Right This Il-10 never had a chance to get off the ground due to lack of parts and the superior airpower of the UN forces. It was captured at Yonpo Airfield (K-27), a major base on the eastern coast of Korea below Hungnam. In March of 1951, FEAF received word that there were two air regiments, equipped with this aircraft, in an intense training programme in Manchuria. This reinforced the theory that the North Koreans were still in the process of building a strong air force for use in the war (*Richard Penrose*)

Left An Ilyushin Il-10 ground attack aircraft, or *Shturmoviki*, captured at Kimpo when the UN forces were moving rapidly to the north with the North Korean Army in full retreat. The Il-10 seemed to be used by the RNKAF in large numbers during the first few weeks of the war. It was on 27 June that eight of the Il-10s tried to penetrate the fighter cover for the evacuation of Kimpo and the F-80s from the 35th Squadron shot down four of them in seconds. Intelligence stated that the NK fighters probably came from the airbase at Pyongyang (*W C Rockwell*)

The 36th Fighter Bomber Squadron commander Major William O'Donnell took
this picture from a FAC aircraft while he was calling in napalm strikes by his
F-51 squadron. This hit from a Mustang was against troop concentrations over
North Korea in the fall of 1950 (*William O'Donnell*)